MY FUTURE LISTOGRAPHY

ALL I HOPE TO DO IN LISTS

CREATED BY LISA NOLA
ILLUSTRATIONS BY NATHANIEL RUSSELL

CHRONICLE BOOKS

SAN FRANCISCO

ISBN: 978-0-8118-7836-4

MANUFACTURED IN CHINA

DESIGN BY SUZANNE LaGASA
HAND LETTERING & ILLUSTRATIONS BY NATHANIEL RUSSELL

10 9 8 7 6 5 4 3 2

CHRONICLE BOOKS LLC
680 SECOND STREET
SAN FRANCISCO, CA 94107
WWW.CHRONICLEBOOKS.COM

THIS BOOK IS DEDICATED TO
MY MOM AND DAD WHO ALWAYS
HAD MY FUTURE IN MIND.

INTRODUCTION

"WE THINK ABOUT THE FUTURE IN A WAY
THAT NO OTHER ANIMAL CAN, DOES, OR
EVER HAS, AND THIS SIMPLE, UBIQUITOUS,
ORDINARY ACT IS A DEFINING FEATURE OF
OUR HUMANITY"

– DANIEL GILBERT, "STUMBLING ON HAPPINESS"

WILL THE UNIVERSE CONSPIRE TO MAKE
YOUR DREAMS COME TRUE IF YOU IMAGINE
THEM? ALTHOUGH WE MAY NOT LIVE OUT
EVERY WISH OR HAVE TIME TO STROLL
DOWN EVERY PATH THAT PRESENTS ITSELF,
WE CAN ALWAYS TRY! AND FUTURE LISTOGRAPHY
IS HERE TO HELP. I HOPE THIS BOOK
PROVIDES THE INSPIRATION AND FUN THAT
COMES WITH PONDERING THE ROAD AHEAD.
YOUR LISTS WILL MAKE A NICE MAP OF
ALL THAT YOU WANT TO EXPERIENCE
SOMEDAY AND I HOPE YOU ARE ABLE TO CHECK
OFF MANY OF THEM.

LISA NOLA

VISIT US AT WWW.LISTOGRAPHY.COM

TRUTH OR CONSEQUENCES, NEW MEXICO

LIST THE CITIES YOU PLAN TO VISIT

INDIA!

LIST THE COUNTRIES YOU HOPE TO GO TO

A ZIPLINE

LIST MODES OF TRANSPORTATION TO TAKE

MAGIC EYE MUSEUM

LIST THE MUSEUMS YOU WANT TO VISIT

KERN RIVER INNER TUBING

LIST OUTDOOR ADVENTURES YOU WANT TO HAVE

BOCCE BALL

LIST SPORTS OR GAMES YOU'D LIKE TO TRY

A CARNY RIDE
OPERATOR

LIST YOUR DREAM JOBS

JOSHUA TREE

LIST NATIONAL PARKS AND GARDENS TO VISIT

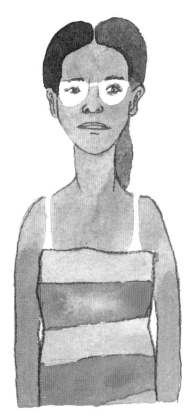

PLAYA BONITA
(REMEMBER THE SUNSCREEN)

LIST THE BEACHES YOU DREAM OF SEEING

DRIVE ACROSS NORTH
AMERICA IN A RV

LIST THE THINGS YOU WANT TO ACCOMPLISH

JOIN A BARBERSHOP QUARTET

LIST THINGS TO DO WHEN YOU'RE IN RETIREMENT

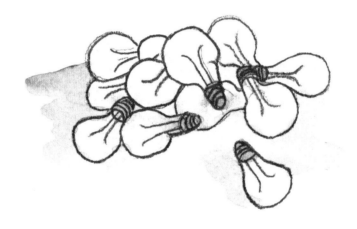

LEAVING THE LIGHTS ON

LIST HABITS TO BREAK

MARCEL PROUST

LIST AUTHORS AND POETS YOU WANT TO READ

LOUIS WAIN

LIST ARTISTS AND PHOTOGRAPHERS
YOU'D LIKE TO EXPLORE

FRACTAL GEOMETRY

LIST THINGS YOU'D LOVE TO BE KNOWLEDGEABLE ABOUT

"LA DOLCE VITA"

LIST FILMS YOU'D LIKE TO SEE ONE DAY

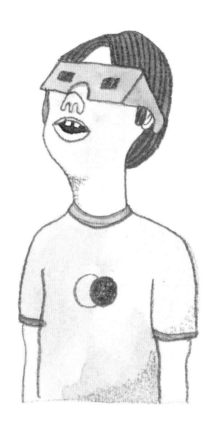

WATCHING THE ECLIPSE

LIST MOMENTS IN YOUR LIFE YOU DON'T WANT
TO FORGET

CYBER-FEMINISM

LIST THE CLASSES YOU'D LOVE TO TAKE

VEGETARIAN PIGS IN
A BLANKET

LIST RECIPES YOU WANT TO TRY

"THE TWILIGHT ZONE"

LIST TV SERIES TO SEE

SNOWSHOEING / WAVE RUNNING

LIST THINGS YOU'D LIKE TO DO DURING FUTURE WINTERS AND SUMMERS

AVOIDING THE USE OF PLASTICS

LIST ENVIRONMENTALLY FRIENDLY HABITS YOU NEED TO START

DONATING TO DOLPHIN
RESCUE EFFORTS

LIST GOOD DEEDS YOU LONG TO PERFORM

"LES MISÉRABLES"

LIST PLAYS, PERFORMANCES, AND MUSICALS TO SEE

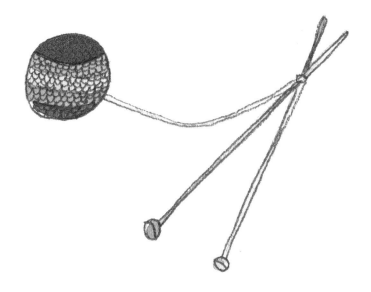

MORE HACKEY SACK

LIST CHANGES YOU WISH FOR THE WORLD

NEW YORK, 2052

LIST EVENTS TO TIME TRAVEL TO (PAST OR FUTURE)

VOLUNTEER TO WALK
DOGS AT THE SHELTER

LIST THINGS TO DO WHEN YOU'RE FEELING DOWN

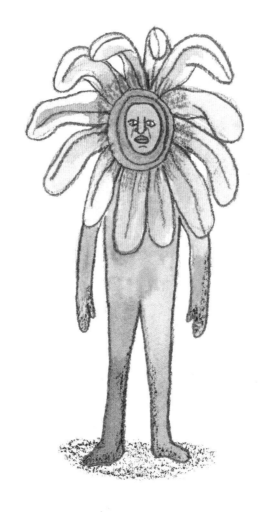

A FLOWER

LIST FUTURE HALLOWEEN COSTUME IDEAS

A GIRAFFE

LIST ANIMALS YOU'D LOVE TO ADOPT

ROCK STAR

LIST OTHER LIVES YOU'D WANT TO LEAD
IF YOU HAD NINE LIVES

LEARN TO LOVE THE
GREEN VEG SMOOTHIE

LIST HABITS TO DEVELOP FOR YOUR HEALTH

EATING MY GIRLFRIEND'S
PLUMS FROM THE ICEBOX

LIST MISTAKES TO NOT REPEAT IN THE FUTURE

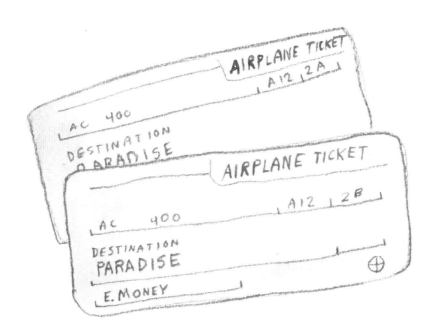

TWO TICKETS TO PARADISE

LIST THINGS YOU HOPE TO RECEIVE ONE DAY

SENSE OF HUMOR

LIST THE QUALITIES YOU WANT TO HAVE AS A PARENT OR GODPARENT

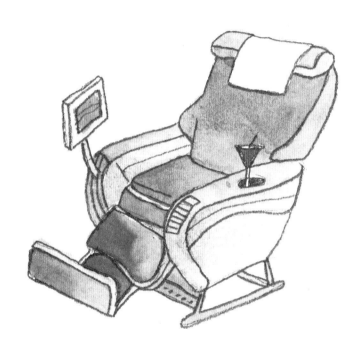

FLY FIRST CLASS
FOR THE FIRST TIME

LIST WHAT YOU'D DO WITH AN ENORMOUS AMOUNT OF MONEY

PARIS

LIST PLACES YOU COULD SEE YOURSELF LIVING

TALENT SHOW AMONG FRIENDS:
"UP NEXT, JAMES'S BIRD CALLS"

LIST PARTIES YOU'D ENJOY THROWING

HEIDELBERG PROJECT,
DETROIT

LIST UNIQUE SIGHTS TO VISIT

LEVITATION

LIST SUPERNATURAL OR MIRACULOUS EXPERIENCES YOU'D LOVE TO HAVE

A CHAKRA CLEANSE

LIST SPIRITUAL PLACES TO VISIT AND PRACTICES TO TRY

SHAUN WHITE

LIST SPORTS FIGURES OR TEAMS TO SEE ONE DAY

THE ELEPHANT SANCTUARY

LIST CAUSES YOU'D LIKE TO VOLUNTEER FOR

PLAY RED LIGHT, GREEN LIGHT

LIST FUN THINGS TO DO WITH KIDS

WE CAN STILL MAKE
A DIFFERENCE!

LIST PHILOSOPHIES YOU WISH YOUR BRAIN WOULD PERMANENTLY ADOPT

PAINT BY NUMBER

LIST ACTIVITIES AND HOBBIES TO TRY

DANCING!

LIST THINGS YOU ASPIRE TO BE FEARLESS AT

DIRECTOR AKIRA KUROSAWA

LIST PEOPLE YOU WOULD LOVE TO MEET

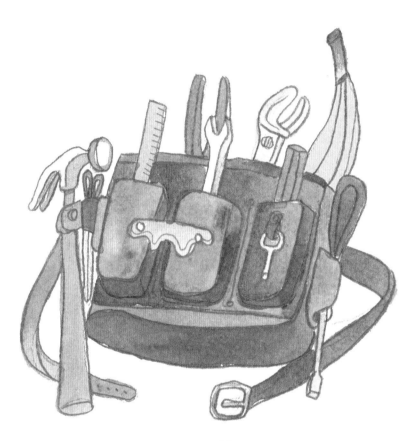

HANDY!

LIST DESIRABLE QUALITIES TO FIND IN LOVERS AND FRIENDS

BEING A BRIDESMAID

LIST EXPERIENCES TO HAVE AGAIN AND EXPERIENCES TO AVOID

LASER TAG

LIST WHAT YOU'D LIKE TO DO FOR FUTURE BIRTHDAYS

DOLLYWOOD

LIST AMUSEMENT PARKS, CARNIVALS, AND FAIRS TO GO TO

WINNIE THE POOH

LIST FICTIONAL CHARACTERS YOU'D LOVE TO HANG OUT WITH

HOLE-PROOF SOCKS

LIST IDEAS YOU WANT TO SEE INVENTED

ICE HOTEL, SWEDEN

LIST HOTELS OR PLACES YOU WOULD LOVE TO SPEND THE NIGHT

DRAW EACH OTHER'S PORTRAITS

LIST DATE-NIGHT IDEAS TO TRY

BERLIN'S LOVE PARADE

LIST FESTIVALS AND PARADES
YOU'D LOVE TO ATTEND

LIST APPEALING QUALITIES YOU'D LIKE TO CULTIVATE IN YOURSELF

A COMPASS

LIST THINGS YOU'D LOVE TO LEARN HOW TO MAKE
WITH YOUR OWN TWO HANDS

ETHIOPIAN

LIST CUISINES TO TASTE

SCIENTIST TRADING CARDS

LIST THINGS YOU'D LIKE TO COLLECT

GRANDMA NEVER WORE
A PAIR OF PANTS

LIST DETAILS ABOUT YOUR FAMILY FOR FUTURE GENERATIONS

BONSAI GARDEN

LIST WHAT YOUR PERFECT HOME WOULD ENTAIL

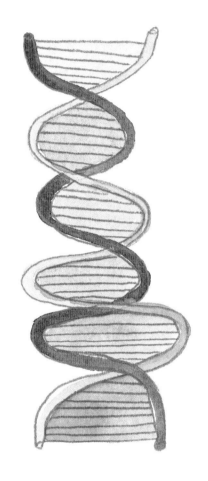

GENETIC PROFILING
GIFT CERTIFICATE

LIST GIFT IDEAS FOR FUTURE GIVING

BIKO

LIST WHO TO FIND IN HEAVEN

MARCUS

LIST PEOPLE TO NOT LOSE TOUCH WITH

THE GREAT MONARCH
BUTTERFLY MiGRATION

LIST NATURAL WONDERS AND MONUMENTS TO SEE

CALLING HOME

LIST SOME THINGS TO BE LESS LAZY ABOUT

PROFESSOR BREITWEISER

LIST PEOPLE YOU'D SEEK OUT AT YOUR SCHOOL REUNIONS

LIST THE LISTS YOU WANT TO MAKE ONE DAY

THE COVER OF
ROLLING STONE

LIST WHERE YOU SEE YOURSELF IN
FIVE YEARS, TEN YEARS, AND TWENTY-FIVE YEARS

A GENEALOGY WEBSITE

LIST THINGS TO EXPLORE ONLINE

ALWAYS WON AT BINGO

LIST WHAT YOU HOPE THEY SAY ABOUT YOU
AT YOUR FUNERAL

HAVE MY FORTUNE TOLD

LIST THE THINGS YOU HOPE TO EXPERIENCE
BEFORE YOU DIE

LIST THE THINGS YOU HOPE TO EXPERIENCE
BEFORE YOU DIE

LIST THE THINGS YOU HOPE TO EXPERIENCE
BEFORE YOU DIE

GOALS

Goals don't have to be big, important things! Just things you want to do ☺ These are some things I want to do most:

- Learn to paint with watercolours
- Learn to sew
- Improve my fitness level
- Become a meditation master

Other things I would like to do:
- Write a book based on my honours thesis
- Write a script for an Avatar movie
- Do some covers of Jem songs
- Maybe start a cover band?
- Learn Japanese
- Learn Chinese (Mandarin)
- Sell my art